To my 2 Best Buddies,
Thanks so much for all your love, support, caring & understanding throughout these past 7 yrs.

God knew I needed you two to help me get through each day.

I value our special friendship & hope in the yrs to come nothing will change it.

Merry Christmas

Love
Kiddo ♡ '93

You Are My Friend Because...

BY JEANNE DAVIS

ILLUSTRATED BY S. D. SCHINDLER

The C. R. Gibson Company,
Norwalk, Connecticut 06856

Published by the C. R. Gibson Company
Norwalk Connecticut, 06856
Printed in the United States of America

Designed by Deborah Michel

ISBN 0-8378-5303-6
GB702

ℐ 𝒞ALL 𝒴OU 𝒻RIEND...

𝒷ecause what we share settles lovingly between the rapture of Laertius's:"A friend is one soul abiding in two bodies" and Joan Walsh Anglund's tender, child-like:"A Friend Is Someone Who Likes You."

ℐ call you friend because of your willingness to be there in laughter and in tears, to give and take diverse ideas and feelings and to be accepting in our differences and forgiving in our disappointments. These are the constants that make strong the beat of our two understanding hearts.

ℐ call you friend because my life is richer for your presence. When I am reminded of our friendship, I think of de Montaigne's response to the question of why a certain man was his dearest friend: "If you press me to say why I love my Friend, I can say no more that it is because He is He and I am I."

ℐ.𝒟.

Friendship is a pact where one balances faults and qualities. One can judge a friend, take account of what is good, neglect what is evil, and appreciate exactly his value, in abandoning one's self to an intimate, profound and charming sympathy.

GUY DE MAUPASSANT

What thee gives to me, may I return in kind. I would give strength for strength, hope for hope, and strive ever to be of use. I shall disappoint and fail. I will pray for another day to try again.

CLO M. BETTES

We cannot tell the precise moment when friendship is formed. As in filling a vessel drop by drop, there is at last a drop which makes it run over; so in a series of kindnesses there is at last one which makes the heart run over.

JAMES BOSWELL

In Gibeon the Lord appeared to Solomon in a dream by night; and God said, Ask what I shall give thee... and Solomon said... Give therefore thy servant an understanding heart... And the speech pleased the Lord, that Solomon had asked this thing.

I KINGS 3:5-9

I have made some amazing friends...You've got those friends, too. I know you do. The real ones — those folks without whom your world would drastically change.

La Fong went to kindergarten with me. That's 37 years for us. He stood up for me when Dark Mark threatened to beat me up. He was my rock after my dad passed away. That summer we played in bands together, sleeping on strange Boston sofas after wee-hour club gigs. He came to my wedding; I photographed his.

Frack, a restauranteur, saw me walk into his place one night with a long face. Startled, he simply said, 'What do you need?' Nuff said.

Remember River... A lovely woman... A friend who has undeniably changed the course of my life. Our relationship can be as strong as a cable, as tenuous as a thread, yet it refuses to break. We redefine it, pick up, battle, work together, and repeat the process. Just the way it should be.

Maybe tonight or tomorrow you should think of a La Fong, a Frack, or if you're lucky enough — a River in your life. Get in touch with them. And please, without slobbering, tell them how you feel.

ACE HOLLERAN

To Be A Friend...

$\mathcal{W}$hen I've seen or heard or thought of something that makes me thrill, or smile, or laugh, or cry, or give thanks or hug myself, or pray, or strain my brain, and I want to tell someone at once — it's you, my friend.

$\mathcal{Y}$ou see, I know you may not thrill, or smile, or laugh, or cry, or give thanks, or hug yourself, or pray, or strain your brain, and want to tell someone at once, but you'll be glad I did.

$\mathcal{Y}$ou will feel along with me and take my feelings into your heart. You'll go 'Hmmmm,' or ponder and exclaim encouragingly 'Really!' then ask wise questions about what I've told you.

$\mathcal{W}$hen I've brushed against something that assures me I am quite alive, but I don't want to be laughed at, or disbelieved or put down yet want to tell someone, I tell you, my friend.

$\mathcal{J}.\mathcal{D}.$

The only reward of virtue is virtue; the only way to have a friend is to be one.

RALPH WALDO EMERSON

Three things must a man possess if his soul would live
And know life's perfect good —
Three things would the all supplying Father give —
Bread, Beauty and Brotherhood.

EDWIN MARKHAM

A faithful friend is a strong defense:
and he that hath found such an one hath
found a treasure.
A faithful friend is the medicine of life.

APOCRYPHA

I praise the Frenchman, his remark was shrewd, —
How sweet, how passing sweet, is solitude!
But grant me still a friend in my retreat,
Whom I may whisper, Solitude is sweet.

WILLIAM COWPER

A friend may well be reckoned the masterpiece of Nature.

RALPH WALDO EMERSON

Friendship is never established as an understood relation. It is a miracle which requires constant proofs. It is an exercise of the purest imagination and of the rarest faith...

The language of Friendship is not words, but meanings. It is an intelligence above language...

Silence is the ambrosial night in the intercourse of Friends, in which their sincerity is recruited and takes deeper root.

HENRY DAVID THOREAU

TO CHU TA

So you're leaving now,
To travel to Wu Ling!
I bring you this gift,
A precious sword,
To speed you on your way.

But, though worth its weight
In purest gold,
Such a gift
Means naught to you and me,
Whose lives
Are but the sharing of our hearts.

MEN HAO-JAN, TRANS. BY HENRY HART

Two may talk and one may hear, but three cannot take part in a conversation of the most sincere and searching sort.

RALPH WALDO EMERSON

Perhaps the main work of friendship is to nourish and sustain the myth of each other's personalities. We believe in each other's strength and by so doing we actually increase it. We stand by and endorse each other's ambitions and thereby make them more attainable. We encourage each other to reach our ideals.

EUGENE KENNEDY

A friend is a person with whom I may be sincere. Before him, I may think aloud.

RALPH WALDO EMERSON

True friends are the whole world to one another; and he that is the friend to himself is also a friend to mankind; even in my studies the greatest delight I take is that of imparting it to others; for there is no relish to me in possessing of anything without a partner.

SENECA

Our chief want in life is somebody who shall make us do what we can.

RALPH WALDO EMERSON

The third basis for friendship is other-love. Here the concern centers in the welfare of the other person. The attention is not primarily on self, or even on the relation of both. Each person is first of all interested in the other. Such love seeks not its own but the welfare of the other. It is basically giving — self-giving... One of the greatest joys in life is to have a friend in whose presence we feel no tension. We are who we are and we are not alone but with someone who understands and accepts us.

The truly interested is more spectator than participant in his friend's life... He, so to speak, watches his friend as though he were watching a drama; he identifies himself for or against his decisions, but he lets him do the playing. He cares what he does and what happens to him but he never wants to run his life or interfere... He is interested in him, believes in him, expects the best of him and this is what he needs. To be able to be passive, a sympathetic spectator at the right time and place, is one of the truest qualifications for real friendship.

The more deeply we come to know our friends the more we want to share with them the hopes and fears, the doubts and faith that represent our true selves. Only as we break together the bread of our deepest loneliness can we taste the purest wine of our friendship.

NELS F. S. FERRE

A friend is a present which you give yourself.

ROBERT LOUIS STEVENSON

I want a warm and faithful friend,
To cheer the adverse hour;
Who ne'er to flatter will descend,
Nor bend the knee to power;

A friend to chide me when I'm wrong,
My inmost soul to see;
And that my friendship prove as strong
To him as his to me.

JOHN QUINCY ADAMS

You don't have to play games with a friend. You don't have to
pretend you are someone you're not. A friend is a person you
can count on... and who can count on you for emotional
support.

ADELAIDE BRY

From quiet homes and first beginnings,
Out to the undiscovered ends,
There's nothing worth the wear of winning,
But the laughter and the love of friends.

HILAIRE BELLOC

ℰYES 𝒩OT ℳINE...

𝒾f I would have a true look at me,
I would, as best I could,
Imagine what — perhaps — you see
In praise of my best-intended good.
      If praise there be.

𝒾f I perceived myself through your eyes,
Would I smile in pleasure
For a friend I did truly prize?
A friend held as rarest treasure?
      If such there be.

𝒾t's said one's best mirror is a friend
In whom one's All reflects —
One's truth, one's mind, spirit — in blend,
One's inner Self, cause and its effects.
      If truth there be.

𝒪, should ever such a glimpse be shown,
Let this Self, as seen by you,
Reflect all that's fine in your own,
All that's loving, faithful, warm and true.
      Thus let it be.

J.D.

DEAREST FRIEND,

$\mathcal{T}$hank you for being there for me through a difficult
time. Thank you for the walks, the talks, and the silences.
Thank you for appearing like Tinker Bell to leave little
gifts at my door (or in my car.) Thank you for more things
than I can list here, but especially, thanks for the gift of
your friendship.

I'm so glad I know you!

All my love.

Gloria

So long as we love we serve; so long as we are loved by
others, I would almost say that we are indispensable; and no
man is useless while he has a friend.

ROBERT LOUIS STEVENSON

A day for toil, an hour for sport. But for a friend is life too
short.

RALPH WALDO EMERSON

I count myself in nothing else so happy
As in a soul remembering my good friends...

WILLIAM SHAKESPEARE

Life is sweet because of the friends we have made,
And the things which in common we share;
...It's living and doing for somebody else.
On that all of life's splendor depends,
And the joy of it all, when we count it all up,
Is found in the making of friends.

ANONYMOUS

What are the odds so long as the fire of the soul is kindled at
the taper of conviviality, and the wing of friendship never
moults a feather!

CHARLES DICKENS

Nay, my lords, ceremony was devised at first
to set a gloss on faint deeds, hollow welcomes,
Recanting goodness, sorry ere 'tis shown;
But where there is true friendship there needs none.

WILLIAM SHAKESPEARE

True happiness is of a retired nature, and an enemy to pomp
and noise; it arises, in the first place, from the enjoyment of
one's self; and, in the next from the friendship and
conversation of a few select companions.

JOSEPH ADDISON

Indeed,
We are advertised by our loving friends...

WILLIAM SHAKESPEARE

A man's real life is that accorded to him in the thoughts of
other men by reason of respect or natural love.

JOSEPH CONRAD

At the appointed time in the evening, Mr. Micawber appeared. I washed my hands and face, to do the greater honor to his gentility, and we walked to our house in Windsor Terrace (which I noticed was shabby like himself, but also like himself, made all the show it could), he presented me to Mrs. Micawber, a thin and faded lady, not at all young, who was sitting in the parlour (the first floor was altogether unfurnished, and the blinds were kept down to delude the neighbors), with a baby at her breast. This baby was of twins; and I may remark here that I hardly ever, in all my experience of the family, saw both the twins detached from Mrs. Micawber at the same time. There were two other children— Master Micawber aged about four, and Miss Micawber, aged about three. These and a dark-complexioned young woman, with a habit of snorting (who was servant to the family, and informed me before half an hour had expired, that she was 'a orfling,' and came from St. Luke Workhouse, in the neighborhood), completed the establishment. My room was at the top of the house, at the back: a close chamber, stencilled all over with an ornament which my young imagination represented as a blue muffin, and very scantily furnished...

In this house and with this family I passed my leisure time...But I never allowed myself to be prevailed upon to accept any invitation to eat and drink with them out of their stock (knowing that they got on badly with the butcher and baker, and had often not too much for themselves...)

I passed my evenings with Mr. and Mrs. Micawber, during the remaining term of our residence under the same roof; and I think we became fonder of one another as the time went on. On the last Sunday they invited me to dinner, and we had a loin of pork and applesauce, and a pudding... We had a very pleasant day, though we were all in a tender state about our approaching separation.

'I shall never, Master Copperfield,' said Mrs. Micawber,'revert to the period when Mr. Micawber was in difficulties without thinking of you. Your conduct has always been of the most delicate and obliging description. You have never been a lodger; you have been a friend.'

CHARLES DICKENS
(DAVID COPPERFIELD)

In friendship... One cannot be the superior and the other the inferior... Once a personal relationship is established the difference between the persons concerned are the stuff out of which the texture of their fellowship is woven...

JOHN MACMURRAY

Anacharsis, coming to Athens, knocked on Solon's door, and told him that he, being a stranger, was come to be his guest, and contract a friendship with him; and Solon replying, 'It is better to make friends at home,' Anacharsis replied, 'Then you that are at home make friendship with me.'

PLUTARCH

Let your boat of life be light, packed only with what you need — a homely home and simple pleasures, one or two friends worth the name, someone to love and someone to love you, a cat, a dog, a pipe or two, enough to eat and enough to wear.

JEROME K. JEROME

The mystical reality at the heart of friendship is more homely than exotic. Its face is that of everyday existence, of simple things whose power comes from people who can look at and share them together.

EUGENE KENNEDY

At the top of my thank-you list is the item headed "My Son's Friends."

These are the people I see rallying to each other's needs but unmindful of mine; talking about their hopes, fears and confusions as they hang around on our living room floor somehow easy that I, in the other room, can hear them, yet leaving me with the picking up to do after they've adjourned. Yet, these are the same people who have watched me totter into the house after an especially hard day of work — mortally wounded with fatigue — who have gathered around, embraced me, murmured, "There, there," and in a kind of role-switch been grownup, supporting ones, while I felt helpless as a child. "I love you," have said these other children along with my own, when no other words could have served.

There is the remembered sandwich fetched for me one of those distressed nights when a girl in the crowd knew I needed food, but would not see to it myself.

Mothers and fathers of my son's friends, thank you for the occasional loan of your good children who, in their intelligence and humanism, speak very well of you.

Son, happy birthday and, again thank you for making me a mother — sharing your friends — I would have been less a person without.

J.D.

A little word in kindness spoken,
A motion or a tear,
Has often healed the heart that's broken,
And made a friend sincere.

DANIEL CLEMENT COLESWORTHY

It isn't so much what's on the table that matters, as what's on the chairs.

W.S. GILBERT

It's a lovely thing — everyone sitting down together, sharing food. So take a moment, before you dig in, to smile at your friends.

ALICE MAY BROCK

$\mathcal{T}$HOUGHTS ON $\mathcal{F}$RIENDSHIP...

$\mathcal{N}$o thought of friendship in association with loveliness of the spirit can resist sweet association with gardens and flowers, blossoms and living things of the earth.

$\mathcal{A}$ dear woman I knew used to sing a song of her youth that noted: "In the garden of tomorrow will the roses bloom more fair?.." and went on at the end to say in bittersweetness, "But I would so much rather, all my love flowers gather in the garden of today...

$\mathcal{I}$ wish I could remember all the words, but they are gone and so is the mother who sang them. Still, how sweet such thoughts for a friend.

$\mathcal{J}.\mathcal{D}.$

Fame is the scentless sunflower, with
gaudy crown of gold;
But friendship is the breathing rose, with
sweets in every fold.

OLIVER WENDELL HOLMES

Flowers are lovely; love is flower-like;
Friendship is a sheltering tree;
Oh the joys that came down showerlike,
Of friendship, love and liberty...

SAMUEL TAYLOR COLERIDGE

Love is like wild rose-briar;
Friendship like the holly-tree.
The holly is dark when the rose-briar blooms,
But which will bloom most constantly?

EMILY BRONTE

And because the breath of flowers is far sweeter in the air
(where it comes and goes, like the warbling of music) than in
the hand, therefore nothing is more fit for that delight than to
know what be the flowers and plants that do best perfume the
air.

FRANCIS BACON

To know of some one here and there we accord with, who is living on with us, even in silence, — this makes our earthly ball a peopled garden.

JOHANN WOLFGANG VON GOETHE

Homesteading was all hard work, life on the prairie was mostly based on weather — was it raining? snowing? Was the wind blowing and howling something awful? As children we spent a lot of time trapped indoors. We made do with what we had — just like our mother and father did and the few neighbors did — we used our imagination a lot.

My mother missed the flower gardens like she had known back home in upstate New York. So, she took to giving flower nicknames to her little ones. Nan was an Iris, John was a Boston fern, the baby Sam was a budlet, and I was her "little weed." She called me that not because I wasn't pretty enough but because I was all over the place at once. Nobody ever knew where I'd pop up or even when!

I made up playmates all the time. They were always little girls like me and they were a lot like me. I mean, they liked to write stories and run out to the shed or to the fields to be alone. One of the happiest days of my life was when a family homesteaded about a mile from our vasty spread and there was a real little girl about my own age and she had yellow curly hair like mine. We took to each other at once, and twice a week her father brought her to us so she could be taught by our mother, who was well educated. We learned the usual reading, writing and arithmetic, but also we studied the

Bible and sang songs. Of course the girls learned needlework too, and the boys learned how to farm and hunt (and fight!) from their brothers, mostly.

My friend's real name was Bessie, but I gave her a flower name so she could be more like our family. She was a sister to me then and later even when we grew up. It took forever to decide which flower my friend should be. My brother John said "Buttercup. Her head is yellow and curly like a buttercup." But it just wouldn't do. If forget-me-not had not been so long and tiresome to say, I would have chosen it.

"How about Lily?" Mother suggested. "If her name was Elizabeth it would even be one of the nicknames for that."

"But my name is Elizabeth," she said. "They just call me Bessie."

And so she became Lily to all of us. One of my childhood poems was called "In the Garden of My Heart." They are all there — Nan the Iris, John the Boston fern, Sam the tiny bud and me, Little Weed. I added Lily, my friend, to the poem.

CLO M. BETTES

Still, in a way, nobody sees a flower — really — it is so small — we haven't time — and to see takes time, like to have a friend takes time.

GEORGIA O'KEEFE

Men will confess to treason, murder, arson, false teeth, or a wig. How many of them will own up to a lack of humor?

MOORE COLBY

Laughter is not at all a bad beginning for friendship...

OSCAR WILDE

A true friend walks in when the rest of the world walks out. You can always tell a real friend: when you've made a fool of yourself, he doesn't feel you've done a permanent job.

SAMUEL JOHNSON

Madame de Stael is such a good friend, she would throw all her friends in the river for the pleasure of fishing them out.

CHARLES MAURICE DE TALLYRAND

Friendship is like a bank account: you cannot continue to draw
on it without making deposits.

SAMUEL BUTLER

I am quite sure he thinks that I am
God—
Since he is God on whom each one
depends
For life and all things that His bounty
sends—
My dear old dog, most constant of all
friends.

WILLIAM CROSWELL DOANE

Friends are quite like cakes. Some are devils, some are spicy,
some are lemons, some are icy, some are nutty, but very few
are perfect lemons.

UNKNOWN

Thrice blessed are our friends: they come, they stay,
And presently they go away.

RICHARD R. KIRK

I fancy when I go to rest some one will
bring to light
Some kindly word or goodly act long buried
out of sight;
But, if it's all the same to you, just give to me instead,
The bouquets while I'm living and the knocking
when I'm dead.

LOUIS EDWIN THAYER

Old friends are most too home-like now.
They know your age, and when
You got expelled from school, and lots
Of other things.

BEN KING JR.

We are interested in others when they are interested in us.

PUBLILIUS SYRUS

The holy passion of Friendship is of so sweet and steady and loyal and enduring a nature that it will last through a whole lifetime, if not asked to lend money.

It takes your enemy and your friend, working together, to hurt you to the heart; the one to slander you and the other to get the news to you.

MARK TWAIN

In all thy humours, whether grave or
mellow,
Thou'rt such a touchy, testy, pleasant
fellow;
Hast so much wit, and mirth, and spleen about thee,
There is no living with thee, nor without thee.

JOSEPH ADDISON

An acquaintance that begins with a compliment is sure to develop into a real friendship.

OSCAR WILDE

True humour springs not more from the head than from the heart; it is not contempt, its essence is love; it issues not in laughter, but in still smiles, which lie far deeper.

THOMAS CARLYLE

I have often thought, that as longevity is generally desired, and I believe, generally expected, it would be wise to be continually adding to the number of our friends, that the loss of some may be supplied by others. Friendship, 'the vine of life,' should, like a well stocked cellar, be thus continually renewed.

SAMUEL JOHNSON

ONE AND ONE...

$\mathscr{H}$ow many years ago was it you first gave me the sum total of what had gone before in your life and I gave mine to you? From the beginning we brought out the best in each other. We right away cared about the well-being of the other. We were eager and ready to share our most private selves, especially in the hope of doing the other some good. From the start, whenever we swam, walked, talked and sang together, laughed, cried, hurt and healed together, it was utterly happier and more successful than doing all that on our own. I think that first time we said "hello" was an important joining of two beings. Time has welded that connection and actually, I believe, created another being, a "someone else." One and one, as always, make two, but in the case of authentic friends one and one make three.

$\mathscr{J}.\mathscr{D}.$

My self is precisely that which I must bring to my friends, with which I must approach them, and through which I must present whatever contribution I have to make. I cannot suppress it. I must find the place with the relationship which it can legitimately fit, and let it grow into it. Any friendship— between two or between a hundred—entails a new emergent unity, where each of the constituent selves is far more in its functional oneness with the rest than it ever was in its apartness.

GREGORY VLASTOS

We are reminded here that friendship — Byron's 'love without his wings' — comes in many guises and is seldom an equal arrangement. As in marriage, one side often cares more than the other, or is more nurturing or more faithful... What then makes for friendship? Verbal communications says the author, [Louis Auchincloss, in his 'Love Without Wings' — Houghton Mifflin Co.] as well as shared tastes, complementary qualities. There is the friend as alter ego — someone, as Colonel House put it, 'with whom I could work out the things I had so deeply at heart.'

NANCY CALDWELL SOREL

Give what you have. To someone it may be better than you dare to think.

HENRY WADSWORTH LONGFELLOW

Friendship does not work when people try to cement their relationship to each other by every legal and psychological fixative. Friendship thrives, like so many natural and human things, when we acknowledge its mystery and give it room in which to grow.

EUGENE KENNEDY

There can be no friendship where there is no freedom. Friendship loves a free air, and will not be penned up in straight and narrow enclosures. It will speak freely and act so too; and take nothing ill where no ill is meant; nay, where it is it will easily forgive and forget too upon small acknowledgments...

Friends are true twins in soul; they sympathize in everything and have the same love and aversion...

What one enjoys the other cannot want. Like the primitive Christians, they have all things in common, and no property but in one another...

A true friend unbosoms freely, advises justly, assists readily, adventures boldly, takes all patiently, defends courageously and continues a friendship unchangeably...

WILLIAM PENN

Funny, how we take friendship for granted, isn't it? But when you stop to think about it, you can read your life as a book. Each chapter has its key friends. A best friend who lived across the street and was a grade school playmate.

A high school friend, someone you could share your feelings about the opposite sex with. Then in the next chapter, your best friend becomes involved with a girlfriend or a boyfriend and you don't. You feel left out. Hurt. And so the personal book of your life continues.

Just for a moment, review quickly your cast of characters— single out those special people to whom you were attuned, who seemed to connect, who would listen to your troubles and care, whose troubles you cared about, who made the world a lighter, brighter place.

ADELAIDE BRY

Behold, I do not give lectures or a little charity,
When I give, I give myself.

WALT WHITMAN

Blest be the tie that binds
Our hearts in Friendship's love;
The fellowship of kindred minds
Is like to that above.

CHRISTIAN HYMNAL

Though Close We Are...

Though close we are—and ever will be—
There come some times when the thing to do
Is stand aside—be it me or you—
To let the other venture free.
I cherish those times—though few they are—
Of friendship's fond, absented nearness:
The grace of distance lending a clearness
To the bond, thus shared from afar.
But, when both our paths do singly wend
Back to the hearth of our twosome-heart,
It's thanks I give for that time apart
That so lights your dearness as friend.

J.D.

Two people are friends because they love one another, That is all you can say about it... This means in effect that friendship is a type of relationship into which people enter as persons with the whole of themselves... When two people become friends they establish between themselves a relation of equality.

JOHN MACMURRAY

Think on this doctrine, — that reasoning Beings were created for one another's sake.

MARCUS AURELIUS

All who joy would win
Must share it, —
Happiness was born a twin.

LORD BYRON

When you part from your friend, you grieve not; For that
which you love most in him may be clearer in his absence, as
the mountain to the climber is clearer from the plain.

KAHLIL GIBRAN

Once the realization is accepted that even between the closest
human beings infinite distances continue to exist, a wonderful
living side by side can grow up, if they succeed in loving the
distances between them which makes it possible for each to
see the other whole against the sky.

RAINER MARIA RILKE

Let there be spaces in your togetherness...

KAHLIL GIBRAN

Shall I give up the friend I have valued and tried if he kneel
not before the same altar with me?

THOMAS MOORE

The body travels more easily than the mind, and until we have limbered up our imagination we continue to think as though we had stayed at home. We have not really budged a step until we take up residence in someone else's point of view.

JOHN ERSKINE

Much that I sought, I could not find;
Much that I found, I could not bind;
Much that I bound, I could not free;
Much that I freed returned to me.

LEE WILSON DODD

When your friend speaks his mind you fear not the 'nay' in your own mind, nor do you withhold the 'ay.' And when he is silent your heart ceases not to listen to his heart...

KAHLIL GIBRAN

Blest be the dear uniting love,
That will not let us part;
Our bodies may far off remove,
We still are one in heart.

CHARLES WESLEY

A FRIEND AT ALL TIMES...

An enduring concept throughout Man's cultural and moral life on earth holds that "A friend loveth at all times..."

PROVERBS 17:17

But we ask: Is that possible? Can we love when hurt, when rejected, when disappointed, lied to? When betrayed? Only by living and experiencing do we find an answer of our own. Both joy and pain haunt the trials and testing, the sharing of the human condition between friends. But where do joy and pain not haunt the days of our lives? Some friends have loved at all times. What beautiful and encouraging examples they are.

J.D.

And let your best be for your friend.
If he must know the ebb of your tide,
let him know its flood also...
And in the sweetness of friendship let
there be laughter, and sharing of pleasures.
For in the dew of little things the heart
finds its morning and is refreshed.

KAHLIL GIBRAN

Ay, there are some good things in life,
That fall not away with the rest.
And, of all best things upon earth,
I hold that a faithful friend is the best.

OWEN MEREDITH

One song leads to another,
One friend to another friend,
So I'll travel along
With a friend and a song...

WILFRID WILSON GIBSON

Friendship is fine work at close range, high-wire work over
open spaces, a great wholeness fashioned out of the smallest
pieces of life every day.

EUGENE KENNEDY

Friendship's a name to few confin'd,
The offspring of a noble mind.
A generous warmth which fills the breast,
And better felt than e'er exprest.

ANONYMOUS

Honest men esteem and value nothing so much in this world as a friend. Such a one is as it were another self, to whom we impart our most secret thoughts, who partakes of our joy, and comforts us in our affliction; add to this, that his company is an everlasting pleasure to us.

BIDPAI

It befell one day... that we came on a discourse of friends and friendship... We said what a fine thing friendship was, and how little we had guessed of it, and how it made life a new thing... Then we remarked upon the strangeness of that circumstance, that friends came together in the beginning as if they were there for the first time, and yet each had been alive a good while, losing time with other people.

ROBERT LOUIS STEVENSON

For how many things, which for our own sake we should never do, do we perform for the sake of our friends.

CICERO

41

De Profundis (From Reading Gaol)

If after I am free a friend gave a feast, and did not invite me to it, I should not mind a bit. I can be perfectly happy by myself. With freedom, flowers, books, and the moon, who could not be perfectly happy...

But if after I am free, a friend of mine had a sorrow and refused to allow me to share it, I should feel it more bitterly. If he shut the door of the house of mourning against me, I would come back again and again and beg to be admitted, so that I might share in what I was entitled to share in. If he thought me unworthy, unfit to weep with him, I should feel it as the most poignant humiliation...

I have a right to share in sorrow, and he who can look at the loveliness of the world and share its sorrow, and realize something of the wonder of both, is in immediate contact with divine things, and has got as near to God's secret as any one can get.

OSCAR WILDE

He that is thy friend indeed,
He will help thee in thy need:
If thou sorrow, he will weep;
If thou wake, he cannot sleep;
Thus of every grief in heart
He with thee doth bear a part.
These are certain signs to know
Faithful friend from flattering foe.

WILLIAM SHAKESPEARE

Large was his bounty, and his soul sincere,
Heaven did a recompense as largely send:
He gave to mis'ry (all he had) a tear,
He gained from Heav'n ('twas all he wish'd) a friend.

THOMAS GRAY

If your friend has got a heart,
There is something fine in him;
Cast away his darkest part,—
Cling to what's divine in him.

ANONYMOUS

Do not forget your cotton days
When robed in cloth of gold;
Among new friends who crowd around
Do not forget the old.

ANONYMOUS

The Faithful Friend

The green-house is my summer seat;
My shrubs displac'd from that retreat
Enjoy'd the open air;
Two goldfinches, whose sprightly song
Had been their mutual solace long,
Liv'd happy pris'ners there.

They sang as blithe as finches sing
That flutter loose on golden wing,
And frolic where they list;
Strangers to liberty, 'tis true,
But that delight they never knew,
And, therefore, never miss'd.

But nature works in ev'ry breast;
Instinct is never quite suppress'd;
And Dick felt some desires,
Which, after many an effort vain,
Instructed him at length to gain
A pass between his wires.
The open windows seem'd to invite
The free man to a farewell flight;
But Tom was still confin'd;
And Dick, although his way was clear,
Was much too gen'rous and sincere
To leave his friend behind.

For, settling on his grated roof,
He chirp'd and kiss'd him, giving proof
That he desir'd no more;
Nor would forsake his cage at last,

Till gently seiz'd I shut him fast,
A pris'ner as before.

Oh ye, who never knew the joys
Of Friendship, satisfied with noise,
Fandango, ball and rout!
Blush, when I tell you how a bird,
A prison, with a friend, preferr'd
To liberty without.

WILLIAM COWPER

Me too thy nobleness has taught
To master my despair;
The fountains of my hidden life
Are through thy friendship fair.

RALPH WALDO EMERSON

But in deeds,
A friend is never knowne 'till a man have neede.

JOHN HEYWOOD

If with pleasure you are viewing any work
a man is doing,
If you like him or you love him, tell him
now.

BERTON BRALEY

Friendships do not just happen; they have to be made—made to start, made to work, made to develop, kept in good working order, and preserved from going sour.

STEVE DUCK

Hast thou named all the birds without a gun?
Loved the wood rose, and left it on its stalk?
At rich men's tables eaten bread and pulse?
Unarmed, faced danger with a heart of trust?
And loved so well a high behavior,
In man or maid, that thou from speech refrained,
Nobility more nobly to repay?
O, be my friend, and teach me to be thine!

RALPH WALDO EMERSON

I sought my soul,
But my soul I could not see.
I sought my God,
But my God eluded me.
I sought then a friend,
And I found all three.

ANONYMOUS

There ought to be a Friendship Day. In some so-called primitive cultures the relationship, with its privileges and responsibilities, is defined and clearly spelled out. It even includes regulations on how the relatives of the friends are to be treated and what responsibilities are expected in that kind of connection.

In our culture, we have lots of fine days: Valentine's, Mother's, Father's, along with the usual Birthdays and Holidays but we don't have a Friendship Day. That's a terrible omission.

J.D.

George Eliot, the Victorian novelist who was born Marian Evans, the controversial rebel who chose to live for a quarter of a century as the wife of a man legally married to another woman, was miraculously blessed with steadfast friends. One can easily imagine her caroling along with poet John Masefield,

> "O beautiful is love
> and to be free is beautiful,
> and beautiful are friends."

The following lines excerpted from a letter to Mignon Burne-Jones (May, 1875) speak worlds of how much she valued friendship.

> "...Your words of affection in the note you sent me are very dear to my remembrance. I like not only to be loved but also to be told that I am loved. I am not sure that you are of the same mind. But the realm of silence is large enough beyond the grave. This is the world of light and speech, and I shall take leave to tell you that you are very dear to

> Your faithfully affectionate,
> M.E. Lewes (George Eliot)

Let me do my work each day; and if the darkened hours of despair overcome me, may I not forget the strength that comforted me in the desolation of other times...

Though the world know me not, may my thoughts and actions be such as shall keep me friendly with myself... Give me a few friends who will love me for what I am; and keep ever burning before my vagrant steps the kindly light of hope...

> Max Ehrman

Changes will befall and friends may part,
But distance only cannot change the heart:
And, were I call'd to prove the assertion true,
One proof would serve—a reference to you.
Once upon a time an emp'ror, a wise man—
No matter where, in China or Japan—
Decreed that whosoever should offend
Against the well-known duties of a friend,
Convicted once, should ever after wear
But half a coat, and show his bosom bare.
The punishment importing this, no doubt,
That all was naught within, and all found out.
Oh, happy Britain! we have not to fear
Such hard and arbitrary measure here;
Else, could a law like that which I relate
Once have the sanction of our triple state,
Some few that I have known in days of old,
Would run most dreadful risk of catching cold;
While you, my friend, whatever wind should blow,
Might traverse England safely to and fro,
An honest man, close buttoned to the chin
Broad-cloth without, and a warm heart within.

WILLIAM COWPER

When friendship binds our willing hearts
This thought affection paineth:
We meet, converse—our hearts unite—
The parting yet remaineth.

LOTTIE CHAMPLIN

We may write our names in Albums,
We may trace them in sand,
We may sculpture them in marble
With a firm and skilful hand;
But the pages soon are faded,
Soon each name will fade away,
And all monuments of glory,
Like all early hopes decay.
But dear friend, there in an Album
Full of leaves of snowy white,
Where no name is ever tarnished,
But forever pure and bright;
In that book of love, God's Album,
May *your* name be penned with care,
And *all* who have written
Write their names forever there.

LOTTIE CHENEY

As gold more splendid from the fire appears,
Thus friendship brightens by the lapse of years.

MARY P. BENHAM

We may describe friendly feelings toward anyone as wishing him what we believe to be good things, not for your sake but for him, and trying your best to bring these things about. A friend is one who feels this and excites these feelings in return... Those then are friends to whom the same things are good and evil, and by wishing for each other what they wish for themselves, they show themselves each other's friends.

ARISTOTLE

Not every love has the character of friendship, but that love that is together with benevolence, that is, we love someone as to wish him well...Yet, neither does well-wishing suffice for friendship, for certain mutual love is necessary since friendship is between friend and friend, and the mutual well-wishing is found in some form of communication.

ST. THOMAS AQUINAS

Why should my anxious breast repine,
Because my youth is fled?
Days of delight may still be mine;
Affection is not dead.
In tracing back the years of youth,
One firm record, one lasting truth
Celestial consolation brings:
Bear it, ye breezes, to the seat
Where first my heart responsive beat,—
Friendship is Love without his wings!

LORD BYRON

One thing is most admirable (wherewith I will conclude
that first fruit of friendship,) which is, that this communicating
of a man's self to his friend works to contrary effects; for it
redoubleth joys, and cutteth griefs in halves: for there is no
man that imparteth his joys to his friend, but he joyeth the
more; and no man that imparteth his griefs to his friend, but he
grieveth the less.

SIR FRANCIS BACON

When to the sessions of sweet silent thought
I summon up remembrance of things past,
I sigh the lack of many a thing I sought,
And with old woes new wail my dear times waste:
Then can I drown an eye, unused to flow,
For precious friends hid in death's dateless night,
And weep afresh love's long since cancell'd woe,
Then can I grieve at grievances foregone,
And heavily from woe to woe tell o'er
The sad account of fore-bemoaned moan,
Which I now pay as if not paid before.

But if the while I think on thee, dear friend,
All losses are restored and sorrows end.

WILLIAM SHAKESPEARE

Acknowledgments

FAIRFIELD COUNTY ADVOCATE, Fairfield, CT. Excerpt from
Curbside Confidential headed *Fast Friends* by Ace Holleran,
Nov. 14, 1991 issue.

UNIVERSITY OF CALIFORNIA PRESS, Berkeley, CA. *To Chu Ta*, by
Men Hao-Jan, translated by Henry H. Hart, published in *The
Hundred Names* (c.1933)
CROSSROAD/CONTINUUM,On Being a Friend by Eugene Kennedy
(c. 1882)

HARPER COLLINS, New York, NY. *Making Religion Real* by
Nels Ferre, published by Harper & Brothers, New York, 1955.

THE NEW YORK TIMES, New York, NY. Excerpt from review of
Louis Auchincloss's *Love Without His Wings*,Houghton Mifflin Co.,
by Nancy Caldwell Sorel in the February 10, 1991 issue.

YALE UNIVERSITY PRESS, New Haven, CT. *George Eliot's Letters*,
edited by Gordon S. Haight, 1985

ALFRED A. KNOPF, New York, NY. Excerpts from *The Prophet* by
Kahlil Gibran

THE PHILOSOPHICAL LIBRARY,INC., New York, NY. Excerpt
"De Profundis" by Oscar Wilde.

Memories of Home, by Clo M. Bettes (Excerpts)

Adelaide Bry, *How to Have a Friend and Be a Friend* by Adelaide Bry. Originally published by Grosset & Dunlap - A Filmways Co. in 1979.